TO:_____

FROM:_____

New Seasons is a registered trademark of Publications International, Ltd.

© 2011 Publications International, Ltd.
All rights reserved.
This publication may not be reproduced in whole or in part by any means
whatsoever without written permission from:

Louis Weber, CEO
Publications International, Ltd.
7373 North Cicero Avenue
Lincolnwood, Illinois 60712

www.pilbooks.com

Permission is never granted for commercial purposes.

Manufactured in China.

8 7 6 5 4 3 2 1

ISBN-13: 978-1-60553-251-6
ISBN-10: 1-60553-251-7

FATHERS AND SONS

Why Sons Always Need Their Fathers

Written by Meredith R. Katz

new seasons®

A SON NEEDS A FATHER...

…who will assure him that the only shoes
he needs to fill are his own.

A SON NEEDS A FATHER...

...to teach him all of his best moves.

A SON NEEDS A FATHER...

...so he knows where to lean
when he needs support.

A SON NEEDS A FATHER...

...to share his sense of adventure.

A SON NEEDS A FATHER...

...to teach him when to lead
and when to follow.

A SON NEEDS A FATHER...

…who believes that time spent with his children is the best retreat.

A SON NEEDS A FATHER...

...who is a lifelong friend.

A SON NEEDS A FATHER...

...who can make his mood soar.

A SON NEEDS A FATHER...

...whose values make him the
man he aspires to be.

A son needs a father...

…who treasures every opportunity
to watch him explore.

A SON NEEDS A FATHER...

...to teach him the mechanics of life.

A SON NEEDS A FATHER...

...who will make sure he can take care of himself.

A SON NEEDS A FATHER...

...to teach him what it means to be a brother.

A son needs a father...

...who is still a kid at heart.

A SON NEEDS A FATHER...

...to help him embrace his heritage.

A SON NEEDS A FATHER...

...to show him that with practice,
anything is attainable.

A SON NEEDS A FATHER...

...to guide him on his path to manhood.

A SON NEEDS A FATHER...

…who will keep him protected —
no matter where he is.

A son needs a father...

...to make sure he strives for the top.

A SON NEEDS A FATHER...

...who considers his family to be
his most precious gift.

A SON NEEDS A FATHER...

…to show him a place where
he will always belong.

A SON NEEDS A FATHER...

...who shares the sources of his
inspiration with him.

A SON NEEDS A FATHER...

...who would rather spend game day with
him more than anyone else.

A SON NEEDS A FATHER...

...to show him the true meaning of teamwork.

A SON NEEDS A FATHER...

...who welcomes any question
on his road of discovery.

A SON NEEDS A FATHER...

...who is always glad to have him home.

A SON NEEDS A FATHER...

...who makes him feel like he's number one.

A SON NEEDS A FATHER...

…who never hesitates to remind him
where he gets his good looks.

A SON NEEDS A FATHER...

...to teach him that it takes a few misses
to get the perfect swing.

A SON NEEDS A FATHER...

...to be his anchor.

A SON NEEDS A FATHER...

...who has a dynamic spirit.

A SON NEEDS A FATHER...

...who gives him comfort that no one else can.

A SON NEEDS A FATHER...

...who will encourage his spirit
every step of the way.

A SON NEEDS A FATHER...

...to show him the importance
of educating one another.

A son needs a father...

...who keeps his heart light.

A SON NEEDS A FATHER...

...who is happy to make the journey with him.